Reptiles at the Zoo

Divide Within 100

Courtney Sullivan

INFOMAX MATH READERS

Rosen Classroom™

New York

Published in 2015 by The Rosen Publishing Group, Inc.
29 East 21st Street, New York, NY 10010

Book Design: Jonathan J. D'Rozario

Photo Credits: Cover Jenny Sturm/Shutterstock.com; pp. 3, 4, 6, 8, 10, 12, 14, 16, 18, 20, 22, 23, 24 (forest) Subbotina Anna/Shutterstock.com; pp. 3, 4, 6, 7, 8, 9, 10, 11, 12, 13, 14, 15, 16, 18, 20, 22, 23, 24 (sign) FooTToo/Shutterstock.com; pp. 3, 4, 6, 8, 10, 12, 14, 16, 18, 20, 22, 23, 24 (pipe) MC_Noppadol/Shutterstock.com; p. 5 WitthayaP/Shutterstock.com; p. 7 (main) Naaman Abreu/Shutterstock.com; p. 7 (fish icon) Alexander Raths/Shutterstock.com; p. 9 (main) Patrick K. Campbell/Shutterstock.com; pp. 9 (icon), 11 Eric Isselee/Shutterstock.com; p. 13 Michael McCoy/Photo Researchers/Getty Images; p. 15 apiguide/Shutterstock.com; p. 17 Sergey Uryadnikov/Shutterstock.com; p. 19 Benjamint/Shutterstock.com; p. 21 Peter Leahy/Shutterstock.com; p. 22 Vozorom/Shutterstock.com.

ISBN: 978-1-4777-4690-5
6-pack ISBN: 978-1-4777-4692-9

Manufactured in the United States of America

CPSIA Compliance Information: Batch #WS15RC: For further information contact Rosen Publishing, New York, New York at 1-800-237-9932.

Contents

What Are Reptiles?

Have you ever been to a zoo? If you have, you've seen different kinds of animals from all over the world. Many zoos have animals from all the major animal classes: mammals, fish, birds, reptiles, amphibians, and insects. Animals in each class share certain **characteristics**.

Reptiles are one class of animals. They're cold-blooded, which means their body temperature depends on the air around them. Reptiles are born on land and have scaly skin.

Many reptiles lay in the sun to get warm and cool off in the shade. At the zoo, reptile cages have special heat lamps to keep them warm.

iguana

Huge Hunters

The American crocodile is one of the largest crocodiles in the world. It lives in Central and South America and on the southern coasts of North America. It can grow to almost 20 feet (6 m) long and weigh 2,000 pounds (908 kg)!

Crocodiles are part of a family that can be traced back to the time of the dinosaurs. Their thick scales, called scutes (SKOOTS), protect them from harm. Their huge jaws and sharp teeth make them fearsome hunters.

The crocodile **habitat** at the zoo has water in it because crocodiles like to swim and hunt in water. Imagine a zookeeper has 14 fish to feed 2 crocodiles. Each crocodile could have 7 fish. Division and multiplication are closely related, so you can check your division by multiplying 7 times 2.

$$14 \div 2 = 7$$

$$7 \times 2 = 14$$

The anaconda is one of the largest snakes in the world. It can grow to almost 30 feet (9 m) long! Even though the reticulated (rih-TIH-kyuh-lay-tuhd) python is longer, the green anaconda is thicker and heavier. This slithering South American snake can weigh over 500 pounds (227 kg).

What do anacondas eat? In the wild, they eat large mammals, such as deer, wild pigs, and even jaguars! They also eat birds and turtles. They kill their **prey** by curling themselves around the animal and squeezing it to death.

At the zoo, anacondas are fed rabbits. If there are 24 rabbits and 3 anacondas, how many rabbits will each snake get? The answer is 8. You can check that answer by multiplying 8 times 3 to get 24.

$24 \div 3 = 8$

$8 \times 3 = 24$

Different Kinds of Lizards

There are about 5,000 **species** of lizards, and they're all different from each other. Some are very colorful, while others are only one color. Some are big, while others are small. But most have a long body and tail, and a small head and neck. They live everywhere except in very cold regions.

Some lizards can change colors. Male red-headed rock agamas are usually brown, but their head turns bright red and their body turns bright blue when they want to be seen.

Red-headed rock agama lizards eat insects. If a zookeeper has 42 crickets and 6 agama lizards, how many crickets can each lizard have? You can use this triangle, which shows how the numbers 42, 6, and 7 are related through division and multiplication.

42
x ÷
7
6
42 ÷ 6 = 7
6 x 7 = 42

Some lizards have **adaptations** that help keep them safe from predators. When a frilled lizard feels unsafe, a flap of skin around its head opens up. It also stands on its back legs and hisses. Sound scary? This lizard is more afraid of its predators than it sounds. It will often run away as fast as possible after its scary show.

To find a wild frilled lizard, you'd have to go to Australia, but there are many in zoos.

Frilled lizards eat insects and other small animals. If a zoo volunteer has 45 insects and there are 5 lizards, how many insects can each lizard eat? You can make a triangle to help you check your answer!

45
x ÷
9
5
45 ÷ 5 = ?
5 x ? = 45

The green iguana can grow to be almost 7 feet (2 m) long. Found in rain forests, these iguanas like to spend their time in trees, eating fruit and leaves.

Green iguanas are fast, and they're able to leap out of trees if a predator comes around. They have sharp teeth and long, sharp tails. These huge lizards don't sound like house pets, but many people try to keep them. They're much safer in zoos, though.

Many zoos feed iguanas salads made of leafy greens and fruits. If there are 56 pieces of fruit and you have to make 8 salads, how many pieces should you put in each salad? Check your answer by multiplying the 2 smaller numbers in your head.

$56 \div 8 = ?$

$8 \times ? = 56$

One of the largest lizards, and certainly the heaviest, is the Komodo dragon. Weighing in at more than 300 pounds (136 kg), this lizard can grow to be 10 feet (3 m) long. Komodo dragons can be found on several Indonesian islands.

Komodo dragons are powerful predators. They not only eat birds and other lizards, they also eat deer and water buffalo! They're even known to attack people. Komodo dragons were only discovered by scientists around 100 years ago.

At the zoo, Komodo dragons are fed rodents and rabbits. If there are 63 rodents and 7 Komodo dragons, how many rodents could each lizard eat? How can you check your answer?

$63 \div 7 = ?$

Super Shells!

Turtles and tortoises have special adaptations. They have thick shells that keep them safe from predators. If they feel unsafe, these reptiles can pull their legs and head into their shell. What's the difference between turtles and tortoises? Turtles spend most of their time in water, but tortoises stay on land.

The largest tortoise in the world is the Galápagos tortoise. It can grow to be almost 5 feet (1.5 m) long. It can live to be over 150 years old!

Though they're big, Galápagos tortoises aren't predators. At the zoo, they eat fruits and vegetables, such as kale. If there are 72 pieces of kale and 9 tortoises, how many pieces could each tortoise eat?

72 ÷ 9 = ?

Many reptiles live on land, but the green sea turtle lives in the water. It has flippers instead of feet and a light shell. Found in **tropical** waters all over the world, the green sea turtle is one of the largest sea turtles. It grows up to 5 feet (1.5 m) long and can weigh up to 700 pounds (318 kg).

Green sea turtles **migrate** to find food and lay their eggs. Because they live in water, you're more likely to find green sea turtles in aquariums than zoos.

Like most reptiles, green sea turtles come on land to lay eggs. A female green sea turtle can lay 100 eggs or more at a time. How many groups of 10 are in 100? Find the answer in your head.

Visiting the Zoo

Some reptiles live in the water, while some live on land. Some grow to be over 10 feet (3 m) long, while others can fit in the palm of your hand. Some are fierce predators, while others have special adaptations to keep themselves from being eaten.

You can visit many different reptiles at your local zoo. While you're there, notice how the zookeepers take care of them. Count different things in their habitats and practice division!

Glossary

adaptation (aa-dap-TAY-shun) A change in a type of living thing that helps it live better in its habitat.

characteristic (kehr-ihk-tuh-RIHS-tihk) Something that makes a person or thing different from others.

habitat (HA-buh-tat) The natural home for a plant, animal, or other living thing.

migrate (MY-grayt) To move from one place to another.

prey (PRAY) An animal that's hunted by other animals for food.

species (SPEE-sheez) A group of living things that are all the same kind.

tropical (TRAH-pih-kuhl) Something that is from the hot and wet area near the Earth's equator.

Index